BASKETBaLL PiX, RoLLs, and RHyTHmS

Rimshots

Charles R. Smith Jr.

PUFFIN BOOKS

I dedicate this to
MOM, **DAD**, *and* **CHRISTI**, *for always being there;*
and to
MY WIFE, **GILLIAN**,
who always inspired and encouraged me to go out, even in the hot weather,
and create something everlasting for our future children.

PUFFIN BOOKS
Published by the Penguin Group
Penguin Putnam Books for Young Readers, 345 Hudson Street, New York, New York 10014, U.S.A.
Penguin Books Ltd, 27 Wrights Lane, London W8 5TZ, England
Penguin Books Australia Ltd, Ringwood, Victoria, Australia
Penguin Books Canada Ltd, 10 Alcorn Avenue, Toronto, Ontario, Canada M4V 3B2
Penguin Books (N.Z.) Ltd, 182-190 Wairau Road, Auckland 10, New Zealand

Penguin Books Ltd, Registered Offices: Harmondsworth, Middlesex, England

First published in the United States of America by Dutton Children's Books,
a division of Penguin Putnam Books for Young Readers, 1999
Published by Puffin Books, a member of Penguin Putnam Books for Young Readers, 2000

1 2 3 4 5 6 7 8 9 10

Copyright © Charles R. Smith Jr., 1999
All rights reserved

THE LIBRARY OF CONGRESS HAS CATALOGED THE DUTTON EDITION AS FOLLOWS:
Smith, Charles R. Jr.
Rimshots / by Charles R. Smith Jr.—1st ed. p. cm.
Summary: Stories and poems about playing basketball.
ISBN 0-525-46099-3 (hardcover)
1. Basketball stories. 2. Children's stories, American. 3. Basketball—Juvenile poetry. 4. Children's poetry, American.
[1. Basketball—Fiction. 2. Short stories. 3. Basketball—Poetry. 4. American poetry.] I. title.
PZ7.S6438Ri 1999 [Fic]—dc21 98-20578 CIP AC

Puffin Books ISBN 0-14-056678-3

Printed in Hong Kong

Contents

I remember

I remember being so small that I wondered how I would ever get that big orange ball into that basket that seemed so high.

I remember beating my father at one-on-one after so many years.

I remember being the last one picked on my old street court.

I remember hitting the winning shot against the team that didn't pick me.

I remember learning how to play HORSE.

I remember my father regretting that he ever taught me the game after I beat him several times in a row.

I remember learning how to play with other kids.

I remember seeing Malik shake his defender to the ground so bad that the poor guy broke his ankle.

I remember running suicides in high school on the freshman team.

I remember showing up first and leaving last from practice.

I remember when I was the shortest on the team.

I remember the summer I grew tall enough to jump and touch the rim.

I remember challenging the star of the freshman team and beating him at one-on-one.

I remember playing with my cousins in Indiana from morning till night.

I remember when my dad could no longer play one-on-one.

I remember seeing my parents in the stands, even though I just played the bench.

I remember being called "big man" on the street courts.

I remember blocking my first shot.

I remember my first shot that was blocked.

I remember the day my mom took me to the 1985 NBA Championship Finals when Magic played for the Lakers and Dr. J played for the Philadelphia 76ers.

I remember going to Disneyland right after the championship game.

I remember practicing free throws in the rain.

There are things I always forget, but when it comes to basketball, there are always many things that **I remember**.

Excuses, Excuses

"I didn't wear my right headband*."*

"I'm not playing well because my shoes *hurt*."

"My game is a little off because my shorts **are too tight."**

"My shoes are too old*."*

"I'm allergic to *sweat*."

"My shot isn't falling because my shirt **keeps getting in the way."**

"I can't dribble with my left hand because my *watch* gets in the way."

"I keep missing because this rim doesn't even have a **net***."*

"I can't make a layup because I'm not wearing my right *shoes***."**

"If I run too fast, I'll catch a cold*."*

"I can't guard him because he *smells*."

"My shot is off because of this hangnail**."**

"These shoelaces are too long."

"I can't concentrate because of all the noise*."*

"I can't run because my socks itch."

"The *rim* **is too high."**

"My balance is off because of my hair*."*

"I can't play because I'm allergic to *concrete*."

"There's something *in my shoe."*

"I can't make any shots because this net **is all messed up."**

The Sweetest Roll

Drive
draw
and dish.
Can turn
nothing
into
a swish
as I
resist
temptation
to let one
pop
from the top
of the key.
Could be
worth
three,
but only
if I make it.
Fake it
then
take it
strong
to the hOle

with soul looking to finish with a finger roll. To the left to the right earthbound legs take flight ready to excite the crowd into a frenzy. Victory— could be— if my finger roll can clear the trees. As I rise high to the sky I let fly my all with the ball as the buzzer sounds and the swish

falls.

Hot Like Fire

I am on fire and there is nothing that you can do about it.

My eyes burn through you, even though you won't shut up as I continue to burn you.

My silence and intensity never change as you become helpless

and more defenseless.

The only competition that you give me is to challenge myself to see how many

different ways I can score on you.

Your weak defense cannot handle me as I entertain myself at your expense.

12 points so far.

60 points is my goal.

Victory for the team and I. Humiliation for you.

10 points to the school of the left hand.

12 points to the school of the fadeaway jump shot.

10 points from beating you down the court for slam dunks.

That's **44** points so far, and we haven't hit the fourth quarter.

9 points from three-point land.

8 points from using my quick first step to get by you and to the basket. Which leads

me to the final **4** points from the free-throw line, because you fouled me

each time on the way.

65 points.

I want to thank you for helping me to exceed my goal.

As you can see, your endless talk and chatter only served as fuel for my fire.

And judging from the score, you just got **burned.**

THE RiTUAL

Wipe the sweat off the face with the left hand first. That's for Mom. Wipe the sweat off with the right hand. That's for Dad. Spin the ball in a quick vertical motion. Dribble. Dribble. Dribble. Deep breath. Eyes on rim. Shoot.

That was his ritual. Every time. The same thing. Left hand first. Right hand. Spin the ball. Dribble. Dribble. Dribble. Breath. Eyes. Shoot. Always the same ritual. Always the same result. He never missed.

As he stood there going through the ritual, the crowd and the other team tried everything. The crowd would wave signs and large balloons behind the goal—yell, scream, and sometimes even blow obnoxious horns. Some of the opposing players on the line with him would wave their hands, talk to him—do anything to throw off his ritual. The ritual was the key. If you threw off the ritual, then you threw him off. Everyone knew this.

Oh sure, he'd missed free throws before. But that was when he was still learning to be comfortable. He'd tried different things, and some had worked better than others, but after a time he settled on what he does now. He told me the reason he did all this was because he needed something to concentrate on, something to help him relax. That's why the ritual was so elaborate. The sweat-wiping-off thing was because his parents came to every game, and that was his code for saying, "Hi, Mom. Hi, Dad. Don't worry about me, I'm as cool as can be."

It was no surprise that with the score tied, one second left, and no time-outs, he was the one at the free-throw line. Sure, he could make free throws, but half of what made him so great was that he knew how to get to the line when he needed to. He had the ability to make guys foul him and to get the other team mad. Sometimes this slowed the game down; sometimes it also frustrated his teammates, because he really just did it to boost up his numbers.

But that was a couple of years ago, when he was younger. Now he's learned to let a game follow its natural flow. But if his team gets down, he knows how to bring them back. A little drive in the lane, a jump-shot fake, a rebound arc just a few of the ways he gets to the line. And of course once he's there . . . watch out for The RiTUAL.

Gimmetheball!

What is he doing? There's only seven seconds left on the shot clock, and we're down by one. The **ball** should be in *my* hands. I can make it. I know I can. **Gimmetheball!** He keeps dribbling, and I keep trying to find a way to get open, so I keep moving. Five seconds left. An eternity. In six seconds somebody's going to be a hero; somebody else a loser. I don't like being a loser. **Gimmetheball!** Round and round in circles I go. Everyone is on me all the time. Try something different. I'll wait in the corner. I'll hide. If they keep chasing me, they won't know where I am when I just stop running. Everybody knows that I want the **ball**, because they know that I will take the shot every time in situations like this. I have no fear. The **ball** hits me in the chest as I square up to the basket. Three seconds left. No time to think, just time to act on instinct. In a split second, I scan the court and see who is where. The lane is beginning to open up as two players race toward me. I put the **ball** on the ground and head for the **basket** like nothing can stop me. Because nothing *can* stop me. My eyes are focused only on the **basket** and what I need to do to get there. Someone steps in front of me. Step to the left. Someone steps to me again. Step to the right. Two players converge on me as I elevate and bring my arm back. The **basket** begins to move toward me faster and faster. The other two start to fall as I keep rising. The **ball** is in my hand, and I'm ready to throw it down with authority. In the blink of an eye, someone else jumps from behind and tries to take the **ball** out of my outstretched hand. But I still have another hand. I put it on the **ball**, my heart in my throat, the crowd cheering in my ears and blood racing through my veins. I slam the **ball** through and release all my energy into the rim. My feet touch the ground again for only a split second as I am lifted onto the shoulders of my teammates and everyone calls me a hero. All because **I wanted the ball**.

School's in Session

Hands **reach** for the **peach**
as I **teach** others that I
can't be touched.
Sweet feet spin on **concrete** as I
dribble to the
beat of my own drum.
Lesson one:
the **pass**.
I **dash**
a no-look
bounce
behind the back
class
that wakes
the students up
fast.
Lesson **two**: I caught
you staring at my **shoe**—'cause
I blew right by **you**.

17

"Please Put Me In, Coach!!"

Come on, Coach, put me in the game. We're down by 20, and **I know** that **I can** make a difference. **I know**, **I know** that last time **I should have** passed the ball more and not taken so many shots, but **I promise** I won't do that anymore. **I can change**. I know that last time **I turned the ball over 10 times** and that even though I was only in for 15 minutes, I made 4 fouls; but I *promise* **I'll change**.

Come on, Coach, please put me in!! **20** points is not a lot, especially since we *were* down **40** points when I came out. **I'm feeling it** now, Coach. I'm in my **rhythm**, and **I feel ready**. I promise **not to hog** the ball and take all of the shots like I did last time, especially not from half-court, even if **I think** I can make it. **I'll listen** to you now, **Coach**. **I know** I didn't listen before, but **now I will**. I can make a difference out there, **Coach**, **IF YOU PLEASE JUST PUT ME IN!!**

meek

His shirt was a floppy, old, raggedy brown sweatshirt. It had so many holes, it looked like a honeycomb. The shorts, however, were a whole different story. The shorts were baggy, bright orange swimming trunks with the draw cord dangling to his knees. Finishing off the package were socks that had no elastic, so they drooped onto his faded green running shoes. Talk about drawing attention to yourself. This kid was truly unforgettable!

Standing at about six feet two inches, he was not only tall but gangly. Since his weight hadn't quite caught up with his height, he moved very awkwardly. I gave him credit for his height, but looking at him, you wouldn't think he could do anything except blow away in a stiff breeze.

So he bounced his ball in, checking everyone out (you can believe everyone else was definitely checking *him* out!), and found a court with a game going on. He sat down and waited to get picked up on somebody's team. Since he hadn't called next, he waited for quite a while.

The guys figured he was no more than sixteen, being as thin as he was. But the way he carried himself was what later gave him his nickname: **meek**. He did look as **meek** as a mouse, walking in so slow and timid. If somebody had sneezed, he would have been clear on the other side of town!

After about an hour, this boy finally got picked to play. Guys were leaving left and right, and he was the only one there. Because he was new, it was obvious that nobody really wanted to play with him until they knew what he could do.

Once he was on the court, though, you could see a little something in his eyes. When the ball went up to start, he went after it. And that was it—he never stopped. A ball in the air? He jumped after it. Anybody dribble too long who wasn't on his team? He snatched the ball. And rebounds? Forget it. As soon as the ball popped, **meek** would be right up there in the air with it, grabbing it like his favorite Christmas toy. And there was a sound. . . . That sound was downright frightening sometimes. He sounded like a lion pouncing on its dinner whenever he went after the ball. He played with such intensity you forgot he was wearing orange shorts and green shoes.

meek didn't shoot the ball much. No, what he did was all of the other things. The little things that make a team glad they picked you. If somebody made an easy layup, who threw the pass? **meek**. If the ball was going out-of-bounds, who saved it? **meek**. Who found the open man downcourt? **meek**. He wasn't flashy, but he always knew how to get the ball when he needed it. It just seemed that he always needed it.

Everybody was playing hard, talking to one another the way ballplayers do, until someone said, "Game."

Of course **meek**'s team won, and I guess his enthusiasm rubbed off, because they played five more games and won those also. As it started getting dark, **meek**'s mom called him on home, much to the dismay of the other guys. He perked up a little bit, gave everyone high fives and "good games," and said he'd be back tomorrow.

As **meek** headed out of the park, he still moved in the same slow, timid way, but I could swear that he looked just a little bit taller.

After watching him play, I knew that boy was a man just waiting to happen.

Fast Break

Fleet feet streak up the concrete to *pull* a sweet **treat** for the **crowd**. The outlet *pass*— *fast*— as the **break** is *on* and I'm g o n e.

A scene from **The Flash**

I *dash* down **court** to **meet** the pass. Eyes w i d e arms out a reverse *jam* is coming **no** doubt. **sky-high** I *fly* to bring the silent **crowd** back to *life*.

No Sole

"Man, these new shoes are killing me," said the wiry eighteen-year-old basketball player. "I think they're too tight."

"Oh, listen to you. Son, when I was your age, we didn't have those newfangled, high-tech shoes that you kids have today," said a potbellied older player dressed in unrecognizable sneakers.

"*New* shoes," chimed in yet another potbellied older player. "Boy, when I was your age, we didn't even have new shoes. Everybody just wore everybody else's shoes. That's why you didn't see too many athletes wearing basketball shoes, because basketball shoes actually belonged to the pro basketball players. There were only so many to go around, so you had to wait your turn to play in them," he added.

"I don't see what any of you are complaining about," added yet an older gentleman, decked out in a suit and standing off the court, watching the game. "When I was your age, basketball shoes weren't even a thought. We had to play in our Sunday dress shoes, because that was the style back then."

"All of you young bucks just need to hush up and quit complaining. When I was your age, we didn't even have basketball, let alone basketball shoes. Any sports we wanted to play, we had to use bare feet. Boy, I'll tell you, things have certainly changed," the oldest gentleman said as he hobbled off his stoop and approached the court.

"You got that right," piped in a voice that was only heard, not seen. "In my time, we didn't even have feet."

The Scorer

Silky smooth **moves** on the **court** *are* wasted *on those* who *can't* **handle** him. *A glide* *A slide*

A s t r i d e *e* *to the side*

A **ball** *fake* a dribble **drive**

to the **left** *as he* **stutter**

steps

through *traffic* like **Magic** on the hunt *for* **2** points.

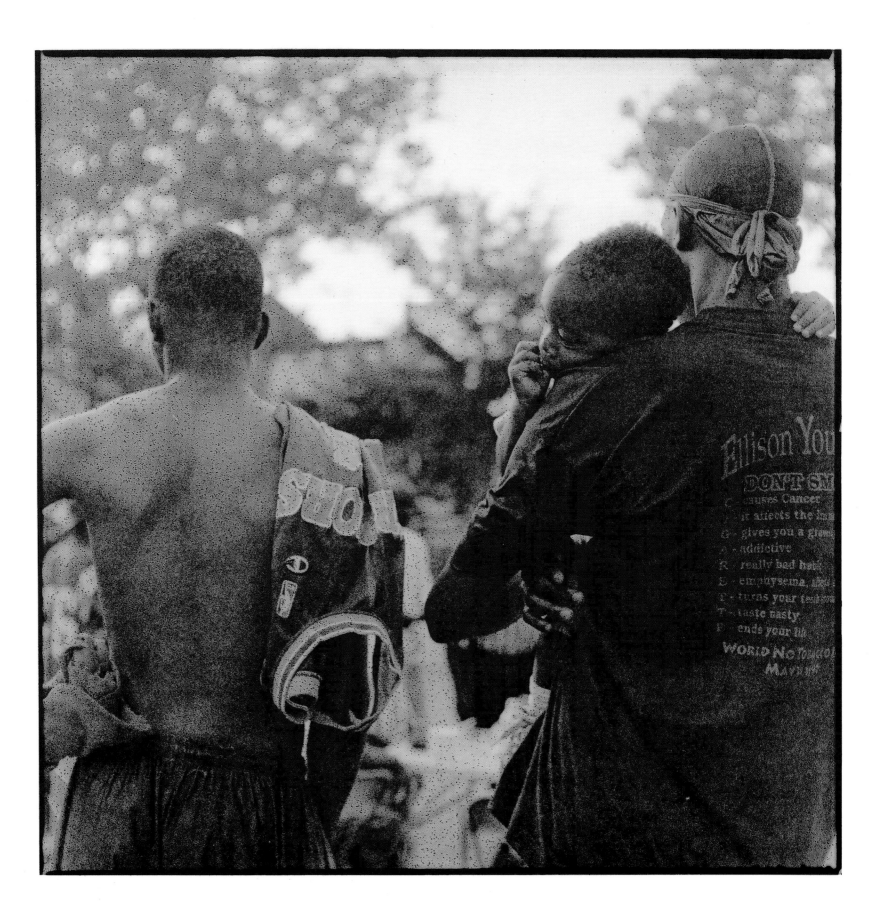

Everything I Need to Know in Life, I Learned from
Basketball

In all my years of playing, watching, and photographing basketball, I've picked up a few lessons to use in life:

Be patient.
Don't force anything.
Let the game come to you.

Focus and determination will always keep you ahead of the game.

Practice makes perfect.

Hard work and continuous effort will be rewarded.

Nobody is ever going to give you anything. You must earn it.

If you don't look out for your teammates, they won't look out for you.

Keep your head up.
Always take advantage of opportunities.

Each person benefits when everybody learns to work as a team.

When under pressure, always maintain a cool head and a calm body.

If you believe you are a winner, you will become just that.

Inspirations

Basketball is a game I have loved since I was a child. Inspired at a young age while watching Los Angeles Lakers games with my **father** and **mother**, I gained a love that is just as strong today as it was back then. Even though I'm not great at the game, I can marvel at those who are.

My parents also instilled in me a love of reading and a curiosity for my history and culture. During the writing of this book, I enjoyed rereading poets and writers such as **Langston Hughes**, **James Weldon Johnson**, **Chester Himes**, **Ralph Ellison**, **James Baldwin**, and **Aesop**.

I enjoyed reading contemporary poets and writers such as **Ntozake Shange**, **Paul Beatty**, **Quincy Troupe**, **Ishmael Reed**, **Walter Mosley**, and **Sonia Sanchez**. The custom of African storytelling inspired me to seek out some traditional stories that featured **Brer Rabbit** and **Brer Fox**, as well as a host of other curious creatures found in a book appropriately titled **Afro-American Folktales**, selected and edited by **Roger D. Abrahams**.

Music is an equally important influence for me because it provides a soundtrack for what is going on visually. No other music does this better than jazz. **Miles Davis**, **John Coltrane**, **Charles Mingus**, and the great **Duke Ellington** are just a few musicians that helped bring my poetry to life. As far as class acts go, there has been none with more style, grace, and elegance than the Duke.

While taking these images on street courts where the heat made no difference and neither did bad rims, I was inspired to try to create photographs as lasting as those of **Roy DeCarava** and **Gordon Parks**. In order to accumulate such a vast number of great images, representing one large body of work, as these men did, I figured I'd better get started and not stop.

Watching a basketball game without great players is like watching paint dry. On the streets, I've seen guys do things I didn't think could be done. In college games, I've seen destinies fulfilled and hearts broken—all within a tenth of a second. Many a night I've spent watching pros such as **Gary Payton**, **Vin Baker**, **Ray Allen**, **Allen Iverson**, **Kobe Bryant**, **Jayson Williams**, **Stephon Marbury**, and **Kevin Garnett** perform with their athletic expertise.

Of course, I have to mention **Michael Jordan**. Known for his aerial artistry and unbelievable shotmaking skills early in his career, he now has proven that to attain greatness is a constant effort. It takes the will of a warrior and the heart of a champion. There will never be another like him, so we should enjoy him while we can. Just remember one thing: Michael Jordan was once a little kid, with hopes and dreams just like **you**.

Raised in Los Angeles, **Charles Smith** followed the Lakers on TV as a child and idolized great players such as Dr. J, George Gervin, Kareem Abdul-Jabbar, and of course Magic Johnson.

After learning **photography** on the yearbook staff in high school, he later went on to Brooks Institute of Photography in Santa Barbara to hone his skills. Upon graduation in the winter of 1990, he immediately moved to **New York** to apprentice with working photographers, learning some tricks of the trade. As of June 1997, he began shooting his own jobs.

Combining his love of **basketball**, **hip-hop**, and jazz, Charles has been able consistently to do what he loves most. He has done work for the NBA, *TV Guide*, *Slam* magazine, Random House, and Doubleday, as well as several other clients. The highlight of his career so far was meeting the fifty greatest players in the **NBA** at All-Star Weekend 1996 while assisting another photographer.

Charles lives with his wife, Gillian, in **Brooklyn**, New York, and can still hit the **three-pointer** from "way out" whenever necessary.